My Mommy loves me, oh so much!

Written By Kat Miller

Illustrations By Ale Tadeo

For my sweet boo-bear,
my mini-me, my little light.

I love you, Lana Rose!

My Mommy loves me,

oh so much!

She calls me many names.

I may be her sugar-pie
at lunch,

then her **doll-baby**
when we play games.

I've heard her call me **angel**
when I'm good and go to bed.

I've heard her
call me **sweetheart**
when she wakes me
to be fed.

My Mommy loves me,
oh so much!

She really, truly does!

Sometimes she says
that I'm her gift,
for no reason, just because!

I have heard her call
me **sugarplum**,

when I roll around
the floor.

I have heard her
call me **silly-goose**,

when I chase the cat
and **ROAR!**

My Mommy loves me,
oh so much!

She sings different names
to me each night!

She sings that I am her **snuggle-bug**,
as she switches on my night-light.

In the morning
I am her sunshine,

and guess what?!
She is mine!

I love my Mommy,
oh so much!

She calls me many names.

I am her precious **buttercup**,
there is no end
to her naming range.

My Mommy loves me,
oh so much!

She really, truly does!

She calls me names,
like **little dove,**

because I'm her baby,
her special love.

www.ingramcontent.com/pod-product-compliance
Lightning Source LLC
Chambersburg PA
CBHW042137110726
48006CB00003B/913